BRISTOL
HERITAGE

A walking guide to Bristol's Churches

REDCLIFFE
Bristol

D0994710

Bristol
RELIGIOUS HERITAGE

CONTENTS

First published in association with
Bristol Religious Heritage Group in 1991
by Redcliffe Press Ltd, 49 Park Street,
Bristol

ISBN 1 872971 41 5

Printed by The Longdunn Press Ltd, Bristol

INTRODUCTION

People who live and work in the city of Bristol do so surrounded by the evidence of their own history. Their business centre is where the first settlement formed two thousand years ago. Their Bristol Bridge spans the River Avon where a wooden predecessor stood in the time of William the Conqueror. And they worship in churches built on sites where once Celts, Saxons and Normans worshipped.

Bristol's amazingly interesting history derives from its remarkably long period of continuous prominence. 800 years ago it became the second most important city in England. It has stayed near the top of the league ever since.

This continuing prosperity has left religious monuments perhaps unequalled by any British provincial city. Bristol Cathedral boasts unsurpassed examples of Norman (the Chapter House) and Decorated Gothic (the Choir) architecture. The cathedral-like St Mary Redcliffe Church is a magnificent example of Perpendicular Gothic architecture. Of the many other historic churches, several are absolute jewels.

Apart from these monuments of the Established Church, Bristol has a great non-conformist heritage. It has the first Methodist chapel in the world, and the Quaker Meeting House in which William Penn married.

It also has a Roman Catholic cathedral that is a triumph of modern architecture.

The intention of this book is to open up this heritage for you. It is divided into two parts.

The first section traces the history of worship in the city.

The second section outlines walking tours of the city and driving tours to the suburbs. There are maps to show the way around the centre.

The two parts are intended to be used in conjunction.

We hope that you enjoy exploring the religious history of our great city.

D.C. Hearle
F.B. Warne
D. Geddes

A HISTORY OF RELIGION
IN BRISTOL

ROMANS, CELTS AND SAXONS

390 BC   Legendary foundation of Bristol by Brennus and Belinus, chieftains from Gaul.

43 AD   Roman invasion of England led by Claudius.

Roman soldiers passing through the port of Abonia, a few miles down river from Bristol, on their way to the fortress of Caerleon on the Welsh Border, tell of strange happenings in Palestine where a carpenter named Jesus of Nazareth died. His followers worship him as God.

Congregations of 'christians' begin to form in all parts of the Empire, even Rome itself. In Britain, house churches meet in the homes of ordinary people and shrines are built in villas.

306   Constantine the Great is proclaimed Emperor at York. He makes christianity the imperial religion.

314   The British church is strong enough for three bishops to attend the Great Church Council of Arles in Gaul (France).

409   Roman rule in England ends. The country is colonised by Angles, Saxons and Jutes from Germany.

425   Irish pirates kidnap a 16 year old boy named Patrick from Aust, on the Severn Estuary. He is the son of a christian deacon, and is sold in Ireland as a slave. He escapes to Gaul and, after training for the christian ministry, he returns to Ireland.

His preaching is so effective that he is soon able to send missionaries to Cornwall, Wales and, under St Columba (521—597), to Iona in Scotland, then to Lindisfarne in Northumberland where a mission is established by St Aidan. St Patrick's followers become the first bishops of the Celtic Church.

580   The earliest mention of Bristol, under the name Caer Brito, appears in a list of 28 towns of Britain made by Gildas.

603   The bishops of the Celtic Church meet Augustine, the first Archbishop of Canterbury, reputedly on the spot where Bristol Cathedral now stands. Augustine is an emissary sent by Pope Gregory to establish the Roman Church in England. Gregory, on seeing English slaves for sale in a Roman market, had described them as 'non

Angli, sed angeli' (not English but angels).

The Bristol meeting is not a happy encounter and the rivalry between the Celtic and Roman churches is not resolved until the Synod of Whitby (663—4) when the Roman tradition prevails.

675—725   Bristol is referred to in the writings of the Venerable Bede.

719   A christian community is established at Westbury-on-Trym, now a suburb of Bristol. St Dunstan, Abbot of Glastonbury, rigorously imposes Benedictine discipline on the community in 943.

720   Abbess Ciolburga, Mother Superior of a convent at Berkeley, takes control of a convent close to the Westbury-on-Trym monastery when her son leaves on a pilgrimage to Rome.

c900   A priory is built on the site of the present Church of St Philip and St Jacob.

1048   Earliest mention of Jacob's Well.

1052   'Brycgstowe' is mentioned in the Anglo-Saxon Chronicles. The word means either a 'gathering place' or a 'shrine near a bridge'. The bridge is at the lowest feasible crossing point on the Avon. Saxon churches are believed to have existed where the ruins of St Mary le Port and St Peter's stand on Castle Park, and on the site of the Royal Hotel on College Green.

NORMANS

1066   The Normans invade England.

1068   King William (the Conqueror) pays his first visit to Bristol and realises its strategic importance. He orders Geoffrey Mowbray, Bishop of Coutances and Exeter and a noted warrior-priest, to build a castle for its defence. The castle is built in the junction of the Rivers Avon and Frome with a moat connecting them on the third side. The Frome and the moat still flow through the centre of Brisol, but, over the centuries, have been covered over.

Bishop Mowbray allocates every tenth stone brought from Caen for the castle keep, to build a chapel at the Priory of St James situated to the north of the River Frome. It is Bristol's oldest surviving building.

1085   Bristol is listed in the Domesday Book as part of the Manor of Barton.

1138	St James' Priory and Bristol Castle are completed. The author of 'Gesta Stephani' writes that the castle seems 'to float upon the waters and sit upon their banks'.

The castle becomes the seat of the powerful Earl of Gloucester, illegitimate son of Henry 1. The walls are gradually extended to protect the town. Four main gates are built, each with a church built above it. One remains: the church of St John the Baptist, built about 1380.

Across the river, a separate township of Redcliffe is established. A chapel of ease in the parish of St John's is built. It now forms the unique inner north porch of St Mary Redcliffe Church.

Another parish is formed east of the castle. It reaches into the King's Forest, an area now called Kingswood. A church is founded on the site of a Saxon priory, an offshoot of Tewkesbury Abbey dating from c 900. The church is dedicated to St Jacob (the Latin form of James), but is now known as St Philip and St Jacob.

1140	Robert Fitzharding, the first Lord Berkeley, builds an Abbey on his lands, now College Green. He brings a group of Augustinian 'Black' canons from Herefordshire to found the Abbey. The chapter house he builds for them is one of the finest surviving Norman buildings in England.

Fitzharding's wife, Eva, founds a women's community on St Michael's Hill. They are called 'White Ladies'.

1147	The original church of St Michael-on-the-Mount-Without is built.
c1150	Knights Templar build their oval church in Temple Fee to be used by retired knights who have served on the routes across Europe used by pilgrims on their way to the Holy Land.
1152–89	The Jewish community is driven from Bristol by Queen Eleanor of Aquitaine, not to return for 400 years.

Judaism is the only other religion represented in Bristol during the medieval period. The Jews take advantage of the christian suspicion of moneylending to provide a valued service to the merchants. They live on the banks of the Frome beneath the city walls in Lewin's Mead. They use the waters of Jacob's Well as a place of ritual purification by immersion in water and the ground on the opposite side of the road is their cemetery.

Queen Eleanor, wife of Louis VII of France and Henry II of England (1152—89), is granted Bristol Castle, Gascony, Ireland and Wales as her marriage portion and administers her estates from Bristol.

1155   The earliest known Bristol civic charter. The first high cross is set up where the four main roads meet, and parish churches are built in each quarter.

1170   Archbishop of Canterbury Thomas Becket, who stubbornly persists in upholding the power of the Church, is murdered in Canterbury Cathedral by supporters of Henry II. His death causes outrage throughout Europe and he is canonised soon after his martyrdom is declared.

1174   The original church of St Philip and St Jacob is built.

1190   A pipe is laid from the Rosewell in Knowle to Redcliffe Hill by Robert, Lord Berkeley.

1195   The first church of St Thomas is built.

BLACK, GREY AND BROWN FRIARS

c1200   The parish church at Westbury-on-Trym is built near the priory.

1215   King John is forced to sign the Magna Carta at Runnymede.

c1220   Three generations of the Gaunt family build St Mark's Hospital to care for the sick and elderly. It is built on Berkeley land facing St Augustine's Abbey. Another hospital is built in Lewin's Mead and dedicated to St Bartholomew.

1227   Dominican friars found a house at Quakers' Friars. They follow the rules established by St Dominic in France. Dominic is a stern and austere Spaniard who demands complete devotion to duty and truth from his followers. His 'Black Friars' take vows of poverty, chastity and obedience.

1234   Followers of the Italian, St Francis of Assisi, settle in Lewin's Mead. A modern office block on the site of their monastery is named after these 'Grey Friars'.

1239/47   A huge engineering project diverts the River Frome to form St Augustine's Reach, a dock which extends right into the heart of the town and makes Bristol a great port.

| 1245 | Carmelite monks settle where the Colston Hall and Red Lodge now stand. The Carmelite order flourishes under the generalship of the Englishman St Simon Stock. Although wearing brown, they are known as 'White Friars' because of the white mantles worn over their habits. The monks make a gift of a water conduit from Brandon Hill to St John's Gate. The water still flows today. |

1298–1333   The Choir and Elder Lady Chapel are added to St Augustine's Abbey. They are designed by the finest architect in Europe (whose name is lost to history). He produces a magnificent and radical 'hall church'.

1299   Grant to the Weavers Guild of a chapel in Temple Church.

1304   St Stephen's church is built.

1313–27   Bristol revolts against Edward II. After being forced to abdicate, Edward is imprisoned in Bristol Castle before being taken to nearby Berkeley Castle where he is murdered.

1316   A chapel which is built on the middle of Bristol Bridge is dedicated to the Virgin Mary.

1337   Edward III starts the Hundred Years War against France.

1340   The present church of St Mary Redcliffe is started.

1346   A hermitage is established on a small burial ground on the corner of Redcliffe Hill.

1348   The Black Plague is brought to Bristol by rats carried on ships from the continent and causes massive loss of life. 'White Ladies' from the nunnery of St Mary Magdalene give help to plague victims.

DAWN OF REFORMATION

1362   John Wycliffe, Master of Balliol College, Oxford, and prebendary of Aust, a village a few miles north of Bristol, condemns Papal teaching. His followers, called Lollards, quickly spread throughout England. They deny the doctrine of transubstantiation and other teachings of the Roman church. Wycliffe is often called the 'Morning Star of the Reformation'.

1373   A Royal Charter of Edward III proclaims Bristol a County.

1388   John Purvey completes and publishes Wycliffe's translation of the Bible into English while in Bristol.

This is the first Bible in English.

1390   Temple Church is reconstructed.

1399   Henry IV begins to persecute the Lollards, followers of Wycliffe.

1455   The Battle of St Albans starts the War of the Roses.

1467   William Canynges, merchant and five times mayor of Bristol, whose money has made the reconstruction of St Mary Redcliffe possible, is ordained a priest following the death of his wife.

1481   Merchant John Foster founds alms houses and builds the Chapel of The Three Kings at the top of Christmas Steps.

1485   Victory of Henry Bolingbroke over Richard III at Bosworth Field ends the Wars of the Roses. Bolingbroke, as Henry VII, founds the Tudor dynasty.

1497   John Cabot sails from Bristol to discover mainland America.

REFORMATION

1517   Martin Luther nails his thesis to the church door at Wittenberg, thus starting the revolution against the Pope's authority that becomes known as the Reformation.

1533   Hugh Latimer, Bishop of Worcester, calls for a reformation of the church and for social justice. He preaches in the Churches of St Nicholas and St Thomas in what has been called 'The battle of the pulpits'. One preacher defending the Catholic Faith leaps about in his pulpit so violently that it collapses and he breaks his leg!

1534   The Act of Supremacy separates the Church of England from the Roman Catholic church. The monarch becomes its head.

1536   Henry VIII dissolves monasteries and other religious foundations.

1541   The chapel of St Mark's Hospital is sold to the Corporation of Bristol to become the Lord Mayor's Chapel, the only civic chapel in Britain.

William Tyndale is betrayed and burned at the stake. His dying prayer is 'Lord, open the King of England's eyes'. A native of Gloucestershire, Tyndale has translated the Bible into English. His mission is to make the Bible accessible to common people. At Little

Sodbury Manor, north of Bristol, he tells a visiting priest 'If God spare my life ere many years I will make the boy that driveth the plough to know more of the Scriptures than thou dost'. He preaches on College Green in Bristol, but eventually has to flee the country and print his translation on the continent at Worms in 1525. He does not die in vain: the Authorised Version of the Bible is largely a product of his work.

1542   The Church of England Diocese of Bristol is formed with the former Abbey of St Augustine as its Cathedral, elevating the town to city status.

1552   The Society of Merchant Venturers is formed.

1547– 1553   The Reformation is completed by the protestant boy-King Edward VI. His opposition to all form of religious ornamentation leads to mass vandalism of church treasures and the whitewashing of church wall paintings.

1549   The Book of Common Prayer is published.

1553   The accession of Mary I brings a revival of the Roman Catholic Church.

1555   Hugh Latimer goes to his death at the stake in Oxford. He wears 'a poor Bristol frieze frock' and, though a frail old man, encourages his companion in martyrdom saying 'Be of good courage, Master Ridley, and play the man. We shall this day light such a candle by God's Grace in England as I trust shall never be put out'.

In Bristol, five protestant laymen are burnt at the stake on the site of Highbury Chapel, now the Parish Church of Cotham.

ESTABLISHMENT, DISSENT AND REVOLUTION

1558   Accession of the protestant Elizabeth I.

1574   The visit of Queen Elizabeth to Bristol is received with great jubilation. Demonstrations of splendour include a mock sea fight in the harbour. She declares St Mary Redcliffe to be 'the fairest, goodliest and most famous parish church in England'.

1586– 1616   Richard Hakluyt the Younger, prebendary at the Cathedral, writes several books advocating voyages to the New World.

1588   Four Bristol ships participate in the defeat of the Spanish Armada. The loyalty of English Roman Catholics is questioned. They can only receive the holy sacrament in secret, disguising their priests as members of their households and hiding them under floorboards or behind walls.

1603 Elizabeth I dies and is succeeded by James VI of Scotland as James I. The new king makes peace with Spain. From Bristol, Martin Pring sails to found a settlement in Massachusetts Bay.

1605 The Gunpowder plot, a Roman Catholic conspiracy to kill the King, fails.

1610 John Guy is appointed first Governor of Newfoundland.

1611 The Authorised (King James) Version of the Bible is published.

1613 William Yeamans, vicar of St Philip's, and Matthew Hazzard, vicar of St Ewen's encourage radical protestants, called Puritans. They themselves contrive to use the legally authorised Book of Common Prayer in public worship, whilst privately sympathising with the independents.

Pioneering work of Matthew's wife, Dorothy, results in an independent congregation worshipping in her house in Broad Street.

1620 Puritans flee to Holland and then to the New World in a ship, 'Mayflower', manned by Bristol seamen.

1625 Accession of Charles I, who goes on to dissolve parliament, claiming that he can do without it. He encourages the conservative religious reforms of Archbishop Laud of Canterbury.

1630 Capt. James of Bristol sails into Hudson's Bay and establishes the Hudson Bay Company.

1640 Broadmead Baptist and Lewin's Mead Independent Congregations are formed.

1640 Charles is forced to recall parliament because of the failure of his war against Scotland. His refusal to accept reforms proposed by this 'Long Parliament' leads to outbreak of Civil War in 1642.

1643 The Royalist forces under Prince Rupert capture Bristol and it becomes their greatest stronghold.

1645 Parliamentary forces, under Col. Fairfax, retake Bristol.

1649 Charles I is tried and executed.

1654 Bristol Castle is destroyed on orders of Oliver Cromwell, Lord Protector.

1656 The Society of Friends (Quakers) acquire Quakers'

Friars.

1658 The authoritarian Cromwell dies and is succeeded by his son Richard, who is overthrown by the army a year later.

RESTORATION

1660 Charles II is offered the throne without conditions.

Dissenting christians again suffer persecution. In Bristol they are forced to meet in secret in the Great Room built over some shops in St James Backs — just as the Baptists meet now over shops in Broadmead.

The Quakers endure harsh treatment for their refusal to take oaths, pay religious taxes, bear arms or conform to the Church of England. Hundreds are thrown into Bridewell jail where many die of disease and privation. Their custom of appearing in the streets dressed in sackcloth, as a sign that God's judgement is about to fall on the sinful city, does not endear them to their fellow-citizens.

1665 William Penn, son of the famous Admiral William Penn, who is buried in St Mary Redcliffe, joins the Quaker movement. In 1681 he accepts a grant of land in the American colonies as settlement of a loan made by his father to the King. He introduces freedom of religion to Pennsylvania. In 1696, he marries Hannah Callowhill at Quakers' Friars.

1679 Edward Terrell founds Bristol Baptist College, which becomes and remains the leading Baptist seminary.

1685 Charles II dies and is succeeded by his Roman Catholic brother James II. Charles II's illegitimate son, the protestant Duke of Monmouth, leads a revolt in the West Country and almost captures Bristol before being defeated at Sedgemoor, south of Bristol, in the last battle on English soil. Terrible retribution follows with Judge Jeffreys conducting summary trials and transporting or executing thousands of rebel sympathisers. Bristol gets off lightly but Jeffreys causes consternation by accusing the Mayor of kidnapping.

TOLERANCE

1688 Parliament overthrows James II and invites his protestant sister, Mary, and her husband, William of Orange, to take the throne. The 'Glorious Revolution' leads to the Act of Toleration which gives Noncon-

13

formists religious freedom.

1694   Lewin's Mead Independent Meeting House is built in Palladian style.

1696   Corporation of the Poor inaugurated.

1708   Capt. Woodes Rogers circumnavigates the world, rescuing Alexander Selkirk, the model for 'Robinson Crusoe'.

1736   Joseph Butler, the Bishop of Bristol, publishes 'Analogy of Religion', which seeks to reconcile the scientific advances of the Age of Reason with the ancient Faith.

1739   John and Charles Wesley come to Bristol and build the New Room, the first Methodist chapel, and begin their evangelical ministry by preaching in the open air. Both had been brought up as high churchmen seeking to revive the practice and discipline of the Primitive Church within the Church of England. At Oxford, their fellows had mocked them as 'Methodists' because they were methodical in devotion, in study and in regular attendance at Holy Communion. Since 1738 they had become leaders of the evangelical revival.

1747   Present Quakers' Friars built.

1769   Completion of present St Nicholas' church.

1771   Francis Asbury, a Methodist preacher, sails from Pill to become the 'John Wesley' of America, and eventually one of the first two bishops of the Methodist Episcopal Church.

1775   Lewin's Mead Chapel becomes Unitarian.

1777   St Michael-on-the-Mount Without is re-built.

1784   Rev Urijah Thomas works to alleviate distress amongst the quarrymen on Durdham Down. The clock tower on Blackboy Hill is his memorial.

1790   Roman Catholics gain emancipation and freedom to worship in public. They open a chapel in Trenchard Street.

1793   Present St Thomas' Church is opened.

RENEWAL OF EVANGELICAL ZEAL AND SOCIAL CONCERN

1803   Alma Road Christian Brethren formed.

1804   Work starts on another massive engineering project to make Bristol viable as a port: the construction of locks on the Avon to create a floating harbour wth a two mile channel called the New Cut to carry the Avon around it.

1816   St George's on Brandon Hill is built in Palladian style to commemorate the battle of Waterloo.

1831   Riots in support of the Reform Act break out in Bristol. The Mansion House, Gaol and Bishop's Palace are burnt down, and priceless cathedral records are destroyed in its Norman chapter house. The house itself is fortunately saved. The scale of the violence shocks the nation and the Reform Act is passed in the next year.

Isambard Kingdom Brunel's design for the Clifton Suspension Bridge is accepted. It is completed only in 1864, four years after Brunel's death.

1832   George Müller arrives in Bristol from Germany. He establishes homes for orphans which rely entirely on prayer to meet their needs. The story is told of an occasion when the children sit down to a meal with empty plates before them because there is no food in the house. As grace is said, there is a knock at the door. A local baker has brought them a cartload of bread saying that arriving for work that morning he had felt a message from God telling him to take bread to Müller's orphanage.

Mary Carpenter, daughter of the Unitarian minister at Lewin's Mead, supports destitute girls at the Red Lodge on Park Row.

1833   The slave trade is abolished in the British Empire.

1837   Launch of Brunel's ss Great Western.

1841   The Great Western Railway from London to Bristol is completed. Brunel is the Chief Engineer.

1843   The Roman Catholic Church of St Mary on the Quay, in classical style, is opened.

Brunel launches the ss Great Britain, the world's first iron-clad ocean-going propeller driven ship.

1844   Christ Church, Clifton, built by evangelical Anglicans, is consecrated.

A revival of faith and discipline within the Anglican church, inspired by high churchmen such as Newman, Pusey and Keble, finds expression in All Saints' Church, Clifton.

1848   A romanesque style building is opened on Honey Pen Hill as the catholic Pro-Cathedral of the Diocese of Clifton, but is never consecrated. Between 1870 and

1876 Bishop Clifford re-constructs it but never completes the project.

1865   William Booth founds the Salvation Army, a military-style evangelical force. Its followers serve the poorest of the poor and open a Citadel in Backfield Road, Bristol, in 1886.

DESTRUCTION AND RENEWAL

1914–1918   First World War.

1940–1942   German air raids on Bristol cause great damage to ancient churches.

1943   Clifton College is used as the headquarters of the American 1st Army, preparing for the invasion of Europe.

1967   All Saints' in Clifton is re-consecrated.

1973   The Roman Catholic Cathedral of St Peter and St Paul in Clifton is consecrated.

St Nicholas' Church is re-opened as an ecclesiastical museum.

1984   Billy Graham conducts a Mission at the Ashton Gate stadium of Bristol City Football Club. 240,000 people attend, 20,440 of whom come forward to bear witness to their faith.

TOUR 1

COLLEGE GREEN

COLLEGE GREEN(A) is an appropriate place to start an exploration of Bristol's churches. It could well have been the place where St Augustine, emissary of the Pope, met the Celtic bishops in 603 to settle the rivalry between the Roman and Celtic Churches. The matter was eventually resolved at the Synod of Whitby, 60 years later.

On the south side and under the Swallow Royal Hotel, stood the church of **St Augustine the Less**. It was destroyed during the bombing raids, and traces of a Saxon graveyard were found beneath it. It may well have been here when St Augustine met the bishops.

THE CATHEDRAL(B) was founded as an abbey in 1140 by Robert Fitzharding. The Fitzhardings were wealthy merchants and one of Bristol's greatest 12th century families. Robert was the reeve of Bristol, a combination of mayor and customs collector. Henry II made him the Lord of Berkeley and gave him the Berkeley lands north of Bristol as thanks for his support in the civil war against King Stephen. Fitzharding is buried at the foot of the pulpit steps.

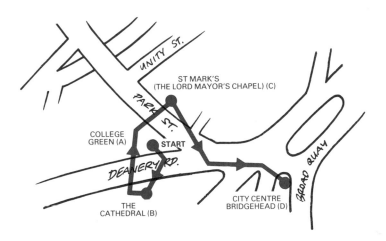

To found his abbey, Fitzharding imported a group of Augustinian monks, known as Black Canons, from Herefordshire. In contrast to other monks, the Black Canons served the secular community in addition to observing the liturgical rules of the Order.

There are still important remains from Fitzharding's time. Two are outside the cathedral. Facing College Green, between the West front and the Library, is the **Abbey Gatehouse** which has a typical round Norman arch. The upper storey of the gatehouse was added in the 15th century.

Through the gatehouse, down the hill on the left, there is an even more impressive **Norman Doorway**. On the tympanum (the inside of the arch), Abbot Newland later added his symbol, a heart with three nails. His nickname was Nail-heart. The door is an entrance to the Cathedral School.

Perhaps the finest example of Norman architecture in the entire country is the 12th century **Chapter House**, which you reach through the remains of the cloister. This is where the business of the abbey was conducted. It has beautiful, and surprisingly modern looking, zigzag tracery work. Notice the wonderful vestibule outside the front door.

The chapter house was fortunate to escape serious damage in the Bristol Riots of 1831. The Riots were sparked by the failure of the House of Lords to pass the Reform Act. The Bishop of Bristol opposed the Act and the mob came to get revenge. They burnt down the Bishop's Palace, which stood alongside the cathedral, then burst into the chapter house and made a bonfire of priceless cathedral records. They were prevented from entering the cathedral itself only by the heroic resistance of William Phillips, the sub-sacrist, who blocked the door. There is a plaque commemorating his courage.

Going into the cathedral from the cloister, you enter the **South Transept**. Here there is other Norman work: the **Night Stairs**, worn by the feet of generations of monks passing from their dormitory to the church.

Also in the south transept is the **Saxon Stone**, found under the chapter house floor and dating from 100 years before the abbey was founded. It depicts an apocryphal legend of Christ harrowing Hell. He pulls a man up by the cross and tramples the devil underfoot. It is one of the finest Saxon carvings in the west country.

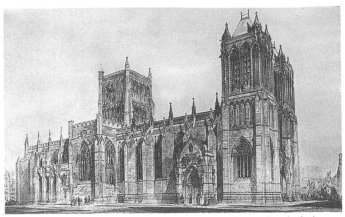

Bristol Cathedral *Drawing by G.E. Street, the architect who rebuilt the nave in the 19th century.*

Walking over to the **North Transept**, you enter the **Elder Lady Chapel**. This is an outstanding example of the Early English style of Gothic architecture which superseded Norman (also called Romanesque) architecture in about 1200. Contrast the pointed arches of this chapel with the round arches of the Norman chapter house. Note also the rich wall arcading and lancet windows and some fine carving dating from 1230.

The chapel was built in 1220 by Abbot David and was outside the body of the church. When the choir and the choir aisles were rebuilt later, two openings were cut to incorporate the chapel into the church.

Move back to the crossing of the nave and the transept. You are standing under the **Central Tower**, which was built between 1460 and 1480. It is a good place to consider the unique **Choir**. By the 13th century, Robert Fitzharding's original church had fallen into disrepair. Abbot Knowle (1306—1322) rebuilt the choir and added the Eastern Lady Chapel, which is to the east of the choir. They are two of the greatest achievements of the Decorated Gothic style, which superseded Early English in about 1275. The architect, whose name is unknown, is considered to be the greatest working in Europe at the time.

The normal way for a major church to be designed then was for the nave and choir to be higher than the aisles on either side of them. A row of windows above the aisles, called a clerestory ('clear storey') let light into the body of

Bristol Cathedral *The Norman gatehouse (J. Trelawny-Ross).*

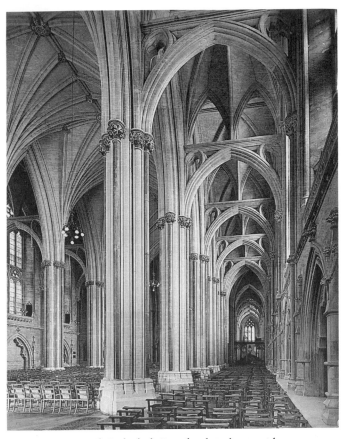

Bristol Cathedral *Central and south nave aisle.*

the church. There is one at St Mary Redcliffe Church (although built at a later date). At St Augustine's Abbey, however, the aisles are the same height as the choir. All the light comes from magnificent windows in the aisles which stretch all the way to the ceiling. This makes the church gloriously light and airy and is the only English example of this style of 'hall church'.

The columns are over 50ft high and support the tallest single arches in England. These arches carry a vaulted ceiling, which was also a radical innovation. The ribs, called lierne-ribs, form a pattern and are the earliest examples in England. The customary style at the time was a long flat rib running from east to west. You can see this traditional style in the **Nave**, which was actually rebuilt between 1867 and 1888. The architect of the nave, G E Street, followed the traditional 13th century practice rather than that of the genius who built the choir.

Underneath the arches in the choir aisles are horizontal beams. These carry the enormous weight of the stone roof of the choir out to buttresses on the exterior of the cathedral.

The **Choir Stalls** were a gift from Abbot Elyot in 1520, though many have since been replaced. The misericords (small supports under the seats on which monks could rest during services) are pre-reformation and are particularly fine. 28 remain, including carvings depicting Reynard the Fox, domestic scenes, a mermaid and a nun at a lectern. Some were judged obscene in Victorian times and removed!

The **Eastern Lady Chapel**, behind the choir, has most wonderful decoration. Before Edward VI had his way, all churches were as colourful as this chapel. The great eastern window is a magnificent example of the Decorated style. Instead of having separate narrow lancet windows as in the Early English period, windows were combined in one 'frame'. The panes of glass were separated by bars of stone called mullions which form a Y shape called bar tracery. There is medieval glass in the top of the windows. That in the centre is Victorian.

The beautiful 15th century chandelier in the Berkeley Chapel.

Choir stall carved with the arms of Abbot Elyot, 1520 (G. Kelsey).

The chapel was probably decorated after 1337 and features the arms of the Berkeley family and other great families associated with them.

Above the reredos (the screen covering the wall at the back of the altar), in arches to the right and left, are carvings of the heads of a King and a Queen. It is thought that they are of the youthful King Edward II and his queen, Isabella of France. In 1327, Edward was forced to abdicate by supporters of Isabella and her lover, Mortimer. He was held in prison in Bristol Castle, before being marched 20 miles north to Berkeley Castle. There, in the home of the Berkeley family, he was brutally murdered.

Edward's 18 year old son took the throne as Edward III. He became famous for his military victories on the continent where he claimed the throne of France. On the reredos are the original arms of England, dating from 1340, as they were before Edward III quartered them with those of France.

Fine medieval stone carvings in the Elder Lady Chapel (G.W.G. Taylor, from Sacred & Satiric, pub. Redcliffe Press).

A parapet above the reredos hides a passage across the east wall. It was built by William Burton, last but one Abbot, and carries the arms of Henry VIII to show that the Abbot would accept the terms of the Act of Supremacy of 1534. Five years later Henry made the break with Rome and, along with all other monasteries, the Abbey of St Augustine was dissolved. Three years later it became the cathedral church of the Diocese of Bristol.

The silver candlesticks which stand on the altar date from 1712 and were given by John Rumsey, Town Clerk. They commemorate a voyage round the world by two ships, the 'Duke' and the 'Duchess', which brought home the castaway Alexander Selkirk. Tradition has it that Daniel Defoe met him in Bristol and turned his story into the classic 'Robinson Crusoe'.

The Chapel also has tombs of the 15th century Abbots Newbury, Hunt and Newland.

The little organ has a chequered history. Originally it was the chaire organ below the main instrument. When the organ was split it was sold and became a bookcase in a house in Durham. A century later it was generously returned and re-fitted with new pipes and stops.

To the south of the Eastern Lady Chapel is the **Berkeley Chapel**. It contains a medieval chandelier, probably the finest in the country. It dates from the late 15th century and may have been made in Flanders. On the top is a figure of the Blessed Virgin and, below her, St George. The chandelier hung in Temple church until it was destroyed in 1940 by fire bombs.

Access to the Berkeley Chapel is through the **Sacristy**, where the vessels were prepared for communion. It has a bread oven where the communion bread was baked, and a very fine vaulted ceiling.

On the lawn outside the west front is a sculpture by Naomi Blake called 'Refugee'. It was erected in 1980 and is dedicated to victims of racial persecution.
Open: daily 8am–6pm.

Across College Green is the CHURCH OF ST MARK'S HOSPITAL(C) (THE LORD MAYOR'S CHAPEL). To quote Collins' 'Guide to English Parish Churches', it is 'for its size one of the very best churches in England'.

The Hospital was founded by Maurice de Gaunt in 1230. Because the Berkeley family provided its endowment, the church was not built facing east as is traditional, but north-east towards the Berkeley lands. College Green was used as a common burial ground for the Abbey and Hospital. The cellars of the Hospital were used to store wine imported from Gascony (Bordeaux). Centuries later they became the cellars of the world famous wine merchants, Harveys of Bristol, and are now Harveys Restaurant and Wine Museum (entrance on Denmark Street). In 1541, after the dissolution of the monasteries, the church was bought by the City Corporation for £1,000. Since then, it has been used as the Lord Mayor's Chapel. For 40 years (1687–1727), it was used for worship by French Huguenot

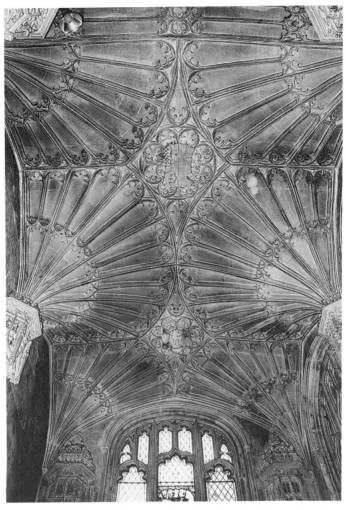

Lord Mayor's Chapel *Pointz Chapel vaulting (J. Trelawny-Ross)*.

refugees, who shared it with the girls from the Red Maids School.

The other hospital buildings were used in turn by Bristol's two oldest schools, Bristol Grammar and Queen Elizabeth's Hospital. The boys of QEH still celebrate Holy Communion in St Mark's Church on Sundays. Their scholars wear their traditional uniform of blue knee breeches, yellow stockings and blue surcoat.

The narrow church is partly of the 13th century, the side chapel having being added around 1320. The east end of the church was reconstructed around 1520 and the tower dates from 1487, shortly after the cathedral tower was built.

A feature of St Mark's is its glass. The heraldic glass in the east window was made for the church, but much of the remainder was collected from France and other continental countries during the Renaissance period by private individuals and purchased by the city in 1820.

Sir Robert Pointz, from the nearby village of Iron Acton, is buried in a chapel which bears his name. He once entertained Henry VII, in whose court was a young man, John Colman, who fell in love with Sir Robert's daughter. Colman was sent back to London in disgrace, but many years later returned to St Mark's as Master of the Hospital. One day he heard the confession of a woman of the parish who was very ill. She died a few days later asking that she should be buried in the Pointz family tomb and that a small package should be buried with her. In the package was a gold bodkin which the now elderly John Colman recognised as one he gave to Pointz's daughter when both were young. In the 19th century, workmen repairing the chapel floor found the body of a woman, clothed in white and with a small gold bodkin attached to her clothes.

The fan-vaulted ceiling of the chapel is an excellent example of late Perpendicular work, and the floor is covered by Spanish tiles.

Open: daily (except Monday) 10am–noon, 1pm–4pm, and Sunday services.

On the north side of College Green is the modern Council House, opened by Elizabeth II in 1956. It is the seat of the city council. The Council House contains a conference hall and council chamber with ceilings of considerable interest and merit. The civic regalia are probably the finest and most historic outside London.

Leave the Green down a short slope which leads to THE CENTRE(D) and the start of Tour 2.

THE MEDIEVAL CENTRE

STARTING POINT: City Centre Bridgehead

Looking from the BRIDGEHEAD(D), you see the remaining section of St Augustine's Reach, part of the former city docks system. In the restored warehouses on the right hand side is the Watershed Media and Communication Centre and the Bristol Exhibition Centre. In another restored warehouse, at the end of the quay on the left side, is the Arnolfini, an important centre of modern art. The Watershed and Arnolfini have excellent cafeterias.

St Augustine's Reach is fed by the River Frome, which originally joined the Avon near Bristol Bridge. Between 1240 and 1247, it was diverted from a point near St Stephen's church to form a straight, open dock nearly half a mile long — a prodigious undertaking at the time.

It was probably from St Augustine's Reach that John Cabot sailed in 1497 on a voyage of exploration, funded by the merchants of Bristol, to find a western route to the Indies. Instead he made a landfall near Newfoundland and discovered the continent of America. A plaque at the bridgehead commemorates this feat (there is also an excellent statue on the quayside outside the Arnolfini). Another plaque remembers Captain Thomas James, founder of the Hudson Bay Company. There is also a fine bronze statue of Neptune which commemorates Bristol's maritime history.

Turning your back on the water, go to ST STEPHEN'S CHURCH(E), which you can see with its square tower rising above office buildings on the east side of the centre. It is the official parish church of the city. The parish boundaries are unusual in that they include two islands, named Steep and Flat Holme, both some way down the Bristol Channel.

A church is known to have existed here in the 13th century, but the oldest part of the present building is the bottom of the **North Aisle** which dates from the 14th century, as do the two recessed tombs and effigies. Most of the church dates from about 1470 and is an example of Perpendicular Gothic architecture. It is a typical medieval town church of the period with no arch between nave and chancel. There are particularly two notable features: the

South Porch has fine fan vaulting, and the **Tower** is crowned with pinnacles finished in rich tracery.

In 1398, Mayor John Vyell bequeathed to St Stephen's a small piece of stone which was said to be part of the Pillar of the Scourging of Christ. The church also contains a memorial to a merchant, Edward Blanket, who is said to have invented the bed covering which bears his name. Bristol was a major centre of the wool trade in the Middle

St. Stephen's (*J. Trelawny-Ross*).

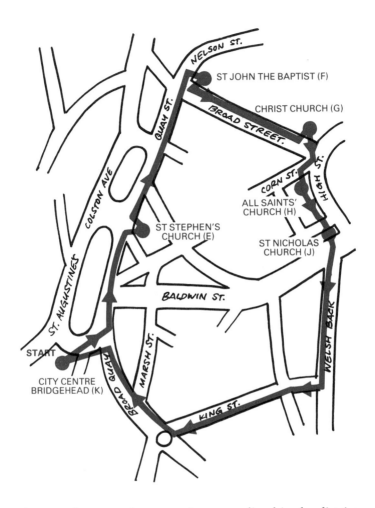

Ages, and many spinners and weavers lived in the district known as Temple Fee.

Another memorial is to the memory of Martin Pring, who sailed to America and discovered Plymouth Harbour in 1603. Later, in 1620, the harbour was the landfall for the 'Mayflower'.

Still in constant use is a **Latten** (a type of brass lectern) from which the scriptures are read. It dates from 1480. It came from St Nicholas' church, which we shall visit later. *Open: Monday–Friday, 7.30am–5pm, and Sunday services.*

31

St. Stephen's *The brass lectern of 1480.*

At the north eastern corner of the Centre is the small church of ST JOHN THE BAPTIST(F). It is built into the medieval wall of the city and stands over a gate which bears its name. The channels in which ran the portcullis can still be seen within the arch. On the city side of the gate are statues of Brennus and Belinus, legendary Saxon founders of Bristol.

St. John's *the archway under the tower, looking into Broad Street with Christ Church in the distance.*

The church dates from about 1380 and stands on a crypt which, unusually, has rib vaulting. Originally it was joined to a smaller church, St Lawrence's, which stood to the south west and shared the same tower. St Lawrence's was closed in March 1580 when the income, which had dwindled to £4.10 a year, was insufficient to support a priest. It was demolished soon after.

The side entrances are 19th century and the coats of arms

St. John's *Bristol's finest 17th century font (G. Kelsey).*

17th. They are those of Charles II, the City and the Merchant Venturers.

The church has a fine **Communion Table** dating from 1635 and a 17th century sand glass by which the preacher's sermon was strictly timed!

Outside the church and built into the city wall is a **Fountain** which is a branch of a conduit installed to service the

St. John's *The late 14th century crypt.*

Hour glass and unicorn. The hour glass was used to time the sermon.

Carmelite friary 700 years ago. It runs from a spring on Brandon Hill under Park Street, Pipe Lane and Host Street, crossing the River Frome under a stone bridge. At election times in the past it was sometimes made to run with wine! *Open: Tuesday and Thursday, noon–3pm.*

Walk up Broad Street to the cross-roads which was the original centre of the town. On the left is CHRIST CHURCH(G), which has a fine Renaissance interior. It was built between 1786 and 1791 to replace an earlier church on the same site, of medieval or earlier origin, and called Trinity. The poet Southey was baptised here. The two **Quarter Jacks** which stand on pedestals above the entrance and strike the quarters and hours, were made by James Paty in 1728 and are rented to the church by the Corporation for twelve and a half pence a year. When the old church was demolished in 1786 to widen Broad Street, they disappeared but were found some years later in a builder's yard in Bath.

Christ Church *Baroque interior with Corinthian columns.*

Christ Church *Opposite: the exterior as seen during the building of the Old Council House in 1824 (City Art Gallery).*

The present church is a fine example of the classic period. There are some well proportioned Corinthian columns and the interior bears a resemblance to London's St Martin's-in-the-Fields. The **Altar Screen** was originally a Georgian altarpiece made by William Paty, architect of the restored church. It has been much altered since and the original texts removed. The **Altar Rails** were made by Walter Swyne who had his workshops in nearby Wine Street. The communion table was also made locally, by William and Charles Court, cabinet makers, in 1790. It has a mahogany

Christ Church *The famous quarter jacks (J. Trelawny-Ross).*

top in the Hepplewhite style and the front panels symbolise the Trinity. The **Organ** was made by Renatus Harris, who also made the one in the cathedral. It has a Queen Anne baroque case and was installed between 1707 and 1708.

The **Spire** dates from the 17th century, when it was recorded that 'Christ Church spire was new pointed, and an iron spear whereon the cock standeth was set up in the old one's place, whereon was a roasting pig eaten'.

Open: Monday–Friday, 7.30am–5pm, and Sunday services.

Originally four churches stood at the cross-roads and a High Cross erected in 1374 marked the town centre. The High Cross is now at Stourhead in Wiltshire. There is a replica in Berkeley Square (at the top of Park Street).

Two of the churches have also long since gone. One was **St Ewens**, once called St Hoyen after a Mercian saint. It was built where the Old Council House now stands. The oldest document in the city archives is a charter of Theobald, Archbishop of Canterbury (1140–62), which confirms Thurstin as priest at St Ewen's, then in the gift of Robert, Earl of Gloucester.

Much later, it was served by Matthew Hazzard, a puritan sympathiser. Matthew's wife, Dorothy, was more zealous than her husband, forming a 'separated congregation' at her home in Broad Street. She owned a grocer's shop and was a formidable lady, leading her 'Amazons' in defending the Frome Gate from an assault by royalist cavalry during the Civil War (1642—1649), though without success. From her pioneer work developed an independent congregation worshipping in Broadmead.

The second departed church was **St Werburgh's**, dedicated to the daughter of Wulfhere, a christian king of Mercia who died in 699. The church originally stood on the corner of Small Street but has now been moved to the suburbs.

ALL SAINTS'(H), the fourth parish church at this crossroads, was formerly known as All Hallows. It stands beside the Exchange.

The western half of the **Nave** is Norman, over which were added other buildings some time before the 15th century. It still has four Norman pillars (though one is a copy). The east end dates from the 15th century Perpendicular period. The tower is Georgian, with a cupola dating from 1807 and is, unusually, sited at the north-east corner of the building.

The monument to Edward Colston, one of Bristol's greatest benefactors, is an Ionic design by James Gibbs, a Georgian architect. The reclining figure was sculpted in 1729 by Rysbrack, who also designed the statue of William III in Queen Square.

The church records for 1407 show that a requiem mass

All Saints' *Charles II royal arms, 1660.*

All Saints' *The tower.*

was celebrated annually 'for all good doers'. After the mass, a feast was held when 2 gallons of Gascoyne wine (costing 8p), 4 gallons of ossey, a Portuguese wine, (costing 3s 5d) and 4 gallons of claret (costing 2s 8d) were consumed.

The church contains an old Bible, the Matthews edition of the Tyndale translation, which renders the 5th verse of Psalm 91 'So that thou shalt not nede to be afrayde for any bugges by night'. Unfortunately, the Bible is not available for public inspection.

Adjoining the west end is a **Glebe House**, formerly used by the Guild of Calendaries (medieval clerks), some of whose records still survive in the city archives. One of these clerks, the 'Black Monk', is said to haunt the church, guarding a treasure hidden at the time of the reformation and missed by Henry VIII's officers. The ghost was last seen by a World War II air raid warden.

All Saints' is now used by schools for religious education and urban studies.

Open: Monday–Friday (School term only), 11am–3pm.

Leaving All Saints', make a detour through the colourful market which occupies the former Exchange, opened in 1743, and the alleys behind. The market has flourished here for centuries since traders were banned from selling in the street. It replaced the Tolzey, where merchants came to meet their sea captains and transact their business. The Rummer Hotel, formerly called the Green Lattis, was given to All Saints' Church in 1241 by the owner Alice Hayle in return for prayers for her soul.

On the south side of the market stands ST NICHOLAS CHURCH(J), the fourth to bear the name. The first, dated 1148, was located on the waterside. The second was built about 1250 over a gate in the city wall, a few yards from the present church. The third was built about 1400 and remains in the form of a rib-vaulted crypt with two aisles and some interesting bosses dating from 1370. It supports the main building and has its own entrance from Baldwin Street, whilst the main church is entered from St Nicholas Street at a much higher level. The crypt is now used as a brass rubbing centre.

The upper church is Georgian Gothic and was completed in 1769. Georgian Gothic architecture had the style of medieval gothic architecture, but not the structural features.

This part of the church was almost destroyed during the 1940 air raids. Services resumed in the crypt in the following year. After reconstruction St Nicholas' was re-opened in October 1973 as an ecclesiastical treasury for the Diocese of Bristol and a museum for the early history of the city.

The exhibits upstairs include a fine display of church plates, robes and vestments. Of particular note are two pairs of 13th century Limoges enamel and gilt candlesticks from St Thomas's church, and a 14th century leather mazer, or drinking bowl cover. Also on display is a changing selection from the Braikenridge collection of 19th century views of the city.

Pre-eminent is a **Triptych** by William Hogarth,

St. Nicholas' *The Hogarth triptych, originally an altarpiece in St. Mary Redcliffe.*

The crypt, now used as a brass rubbing centre.

originally painted as an altarpiece for St Mary Redcliffe in 1756. Hogarth is best known for his satirical paintings, but he always had pretensions to emulate the Italian Renaissance masters, and the triptych reflects this ambition.

As you leave, take a look at the clock in the **Tower**. By Paine of London, it is reputed to be the only church clock with a seconds hand. The church records contain an instruction, dated 1841, that the suffragan was to 'ring curfew with one bell', a sign that the gates were to be closed and citizens were to remain indoors. The curfew still rings out over Bristol at 9.00 pm each night.

Open: uncertain hours, because of staff shortages. Telephone City Museum (223571) to check.

St Nicholas' stands beside Bristol Bridge, the original crossing place over the River Avon. The first bridge was of timber. It was replaced by a stone bridge on which stood a chapel dedicated to the Virgin Mary in 1316.

Cross Baldwin Street and follow the Welsh Back along the water. You might want to continue straight ahead and join Tour 3 at St Mary Redcliffe Church. Otherwise, take the second turning on the right into King Street. On the corner stands the Llandoger Trow (1664), a timbered inn named after the small sailing ships, or 'trows', which brought coal from South Wales.

Further down King Street is the Theatre Royal, opened in 1766 and the oldest theatre in England to operate under Royal Charter. It is the finest example of Georgian theatre architecture in England. Then, also on the right, is the Old Library, opened in 1740.

At the end of the street take time to read the verses displayed on the walls of the 15th century Seamen's Almshouses.

The tour ends back at the Centre.

REDCLIFFE, TEMPLE AND CASTLE GREEN

STARTING POINT: City Centre Bridgehead

Over the road from the Bridgehead stands a statue of Isambard Kingdom Brunel, designer of the Clifton Suspension Bridge, the Great Western Railway and the Atlantic steamships 'Great Western' and 'Great Britain'. The latter is under restoration in the City Docks and is well worth a visit, perhaps by one of the passenger launches which start from the Bridgehead.

Cross Prince Street Roundabout and enter Queen Square, named in honour of Queen Anne, who visited Bristol in 1702. The area was originally called 'The Marsh'. The exceptional equestrian statue at the centre is of William III and is by Rysbrack.

The first house built in the square was No 27, St Nicholas Vicarage, built for the Rev John Reade in 1699. No 37 was the first American consulate in Europe. Queen Square was the scene of the worst of the riots caused by the failure of the House of Lords to pass the Reform Act in 1831. The Mansion House, official residence of the Lord Mayor, was occupied and burnt down.

Crossing the docks, you pass a garden on the right. It is on the site of a hermitage established in 1346 and later used as a burial ground. The towering spire ahead will guide you to ST MARY REDCLIFFE(L). In 1574, Queen Elizabeth I called St Mary Redcliffe 'the fairest, the goodliest and most famous parish church in England'. Looking at the outside, you can begin to imagine why. Actually, some years before Elizabeth's visit, the spire collapsed and remained a stump until the present one was built around 1874.

The church started as a shrine to which seamen paid homage before and after their journeys. This shrine, dating from about 1150, now forms the **Inner North Porch** which you walk through on the way into the church.

In front of the shrine, a magnificent and unique vaulted **Outer Porch** was built in the Decorated Gothic style of the 14th century. Above it is a muniment room where the poet Chatterton claimed that he had discovered manuscripts by a medieval poet called Rowley. He had actually written them himself.

Chatterton was born in 1752 in a school house which still stands on the opposite side of Temple Way from St Mary Redcliffe Church. The precocious boy poet committed suicide in London aged only 18 years. His story was popularised as a romantic tragedy by the Lakeland poets Southey, Coleridge and Wordsworth, who met in Bristol. Southey and Coleridge were both married at St Mary Redcliffe within a month of each other in 1785.

St Mary Redcliffe is most memorable, however, for the soaring Perpendicular Gothic architecture of the body of the church. The objective of Perpendicular architecture was to construct massive 'walls of glass'. St Mary Redcliffe is one of the best examples of how this was achieved. The heavy stone roof is not supported by the internal walls but by the 'flying buttresses' on the outside of the church which carry the weight outwards and then downwards. Since most of the weight is carried by these buttresses, the internal columns can be very slender and tall and the space between them can be filled with glass. (At the Exploratory Hands–on

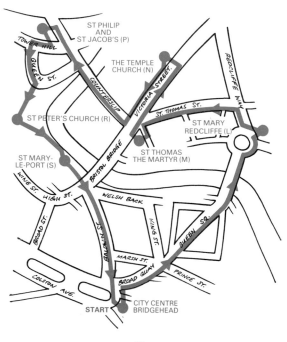

St. Mary Redcliffe *Exterior from south east (G. Kelsey).*

Science Museum, at nearby Temple Meads Railway Station, there is a demonstration of how this works).

The construction of the main part of the current church began in 1340. To the main central aisle were added double-aisled transepts, a long chancel, and the Eastern Lady Chapel. The work was completed by 1400 and was largely financed by a wealthy merchant, William Canynges.

The greatest glory of the church resulted from further rebuilding work by the grandson of Canynges, also called William, in the middle of the 15th century. He added the magnificent row of windows at 1st floor level called the clerestory, and a vaulted roof with 1200 ornamental bosses. Each of the bosses is different and coated with gold. One is in the form of a maze, the design of which was copied to construct a water fountain at Bristol's Victoria Park.

There are two effigies of the younger Canynges in the south transept. The first is very ornate and shows him lying next to his wife, Joanna, who died in 1467. When Joanna died, Canynges was so heartbroken that he gave up his

This 1830 engraving shows the church before its spire was reinstated.

wealth to become a priest. This meant that he could not be buried with his wife, so there is another effigy showing him in a simple priest's outfit.

In his memory, a sermon is preached each year on Whit Sunday before the Lord Mayor, Aldermen, Councillors, and other distinguished guests. All the dignitaries carry posies of flowers, as judges do, to ward off gaol fever. The church aisles are strewn with rushes brought from Sedgemoor to commemorate the entry of Jesus into Jerusalem. The day is called Rush Sunday, and was instituted in 1494 by William Spencer, mayor.

Amongst the church furniture is a **Brass Lectern**, the gift of Churchwarden James Wathan in 1638. He was a local pin-maker by trade. The **Font** is of white marble and was carved by Thomas Paty in 1755. An **Iron Gate** under one of the tower arches is by Edney, a noted local smith. It formerly stood at the entrance to the church and bears the arms of the City of Bristol. There is other ironwork by

St. Mary Redcliffe *The interior: James Johnson's watercolour drawing, 1828.*

14th century outer doorway to the North Porch.

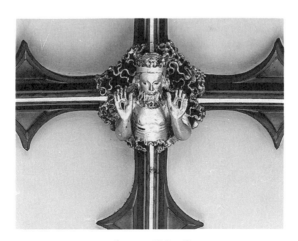

One of 1,200 gilded roof bosses.

49

Edney at the east end of the south aisle. In the **'American Chapel'** at the north-west end, there is a whale-bone supposedly brought back to Bristol by Cabot in 1497.

Of the tombs, one is that of Joan Broke, daughter of Richard ap Meryk ('ap' is Welsh for 'son of'). One of Meryk's duties was to pay a pension granted by Henry VIII to Cabot and it is said that the name 'America' was used by Cabot as a mark of their friendship. There is also the tomb of Admiral Penn, father of William Penn, founder of Pennsylvania.

In the Churchyard is a memorial to the church cat, who lived there from 1912 to 1927, and near one of the paths a steel girder is embedded in the grass just as it fell from the skies during a World War II air raid.

Open: daily, 8am–5pm.

Leaving St Mary Redcliffe, cross Redcliffe Way, where you will see the schoolhouse where Chatterton lived. Walk down St Thomas Street to the church of ST THOMAS THE MARTYR(M) (at present closed to the public). The original church was built as early as 1200, dedicated to Thomas Becket, who was murdered in Canterbury Cathedral in 1170. Though much restored, the north-west tower dates from the original building.

In 1789—1793, the main part was replaced by the present building. The Georgian interior is particularly interesting with a barrel vault and clerestory windows. The coffered sanctuary ceiling was decorated between 1971 and 1972.

Sir William Penn was baptised in the church, and Handel frequently played the organ and composed parts of his oratorios here.

Not open to the public.

Across Victoria Street stand the ruins of TEMPLE CHURCH(N). In 1147, Robert of Gloucester granted land to the Knights Templar who built an oval church, as was their custom. The foundations can be traced below the present building, which was built by the Knights of St John who followed after the Templars were disbanded.

The church was built in the early Perpendicular style. The surviving west doorway was built in the 18th century in the baroque style.

Temple was also the home of the Guild of Weavers and legend has it that the tower, built in 1460, leans so much because it was built on woolsacks. The true cause is more

Temple *The leaning tower (J. Trelawny-Ross).*

likely to be the soft alluvial soil. About 1450, the upper part
of the tower was added at a lesser inclination than the base,
probably as an attempt to compensate. During the 1940 air
raids a Royal Engineer officer was, only with difficulty,
dissuaded from ordering the demolition of an apparently
dangerous building. He needed persuasion that it had been
like that for 480 years!

Go down Counterslip and across St Philip's Bridge. Next
to the Central Health Clinic stands the church of ST PHILIP

AND ST JACOB(P), the oldest church in the city still in use. It is known affectionately as 'PIP 'N JAY'. The earliest certain date is 1174, when it was known as St Jacob-in-the-Market, but it was almost certainly part of a small Benedictine priory established in about 900. The church stood outside the city walls 'within a bowshot of the castle's eastern gate'.

In 1279, Peter de la Mere, Constable of the Castle, arrested and then executed William de Lay whilst he was claiming sanctuary in the church. As punishment for this transgression, the Constable was sentenced to walk from Lewin's Mead, naked except for his breeches and shirt, on four market days, to receive discipline by whipping, and to build a stone cross at which he had to feed 100 poor persons.

The present church was originally built in the shape of a cross and dates from the early 13th century, although it is much altered since then. The **South Transept** consists of a vaulted Early English tower with arches and windows like those in Wells Cathedral. Its eight bells date from 1789. An arch once led from the north aisle into a transept but has now gone. Most of the rest of the church dates from the 15th and 16th centuries and is a good example of late Gothic work.

The **Nave** was much altered during the 1830s but retained its wagon roof and carved wooden bosses. It is made of the original oak given by Richard II, dating from about 1390. No two of the bosses or the stone corbels are alike. Over the north-west door hang the Royal Arms of Queen Anne.

The **Pews** date from 1876 when the original high pews were removed. The **Pulpit** was made in 1631 and was later mounted on the stone plinth on which it now stands. It is carved with a row of bare-breasted female busts, two of which sport bearded male heads! The **Font**, which formerly stood in the south west corner, has a fixed Jacobean canopy dating from 1636. On Sunday 25th June 1857, an astonishing 138 children were baptised in one day! This was probably because the Registration Act came into effect the following day.

The marriage register for 1604 records the ninth marriage of Thomas Coppye, who already had 26 children by his eight previous wives. In 1643, after the Royalists captured Bristol, the church accounts refer to the purchase of

St. Philip & St. Jacob's *The pulpit, 1631.*

rosemary to cleanse the building after its occupation by the parliamentary army. Records of 1688 give details of the collection of 'chimny money' at the Lawford Gate on the Feast of St Philip and St James. The word 'chimny' was derived from the French 'chemin', meaning a road. The tax was a kind of toll charge on travellers.

In recent years, Pip 'n Jay has enjoyed a new burst of spiritual life and activity. A large congregation gathers from places far beyond the limits of its small parish. They are attracted by an exciting form of charismatic worship and bible-centred teaching.

Open: Tuesday and Thursday, 12 noon–2pm (lunches are served). Sunday 10am–6.30pm. Also open by appointment (tel 243169).

From St Philip and St Jacob cross the open space of Castle Green, where Bristol Castle stood until demolished on the orders of Oliver Cromwell. Fragments of the entrance to the royal apartments are incorporated in a restaurant, all that remains of a major fortress.

The walkway along the water skirts around an inlet which is where the castle moat joins the River. The moat runs underground from there, around in front of the Holiday Inn, before joining the River Frome (also underground) at the junction of Broad Weir and Lower Castle Street. This moat ensured that the castle was surrounded by water.

Two ruined churches stand on Castle Green. Both were victims of the air raids. ST PETER'S(R), was said by Simon, Bishop of Worcester (1125—50) to be the oldest religious foundation in the town. The lower section of the tower is certainly Norman and the north aisle is narrow, a characteristic of Norman churches. The rest of the building is early Perpendicular, probably dating from 1400.

When King Edmund the Grand (940—946), a Saxon King, was murdered in the King's Wood at Pucklechurch, east of Bristol, his body rested at St Peter's on its way to burial at Glastonbury Abbey.

During the Civil War (1643—45) the Parliamentary commander of Bristol Castle was a Colonel Fiennes, a lawyer known irreverently as 'Old Subtlety'. As the Royalists drew near he ordered St Peter's to be demolished, since it impeded the garrison's field of fire. He was persuaded to change his orders and, in the end, surrendered the castle after a faint-hearted fight. The church stood for almost another 300 years before enemy aircraft achieved what the not-so-gallant colonel had intended.

The second ruined church, ST MARY-LE-PORT(S), was originally for seamen. There are traces of Norman stonework among the ruins, but it was mainly late medieval. The tower is Perpendicular and dates from the 15th century. It is a good example of the Bristol practice of making the pinnacle which stands above the stair head much higher than the other three. St Stephen's is another example of this local custom.

At this point you can either return to the Centre (down Corn Street or Baldwin Street) or proceed direct to Tour 4.

TOUR 4

BROADMEAD

Leaving Castle Green at the north-east corner, go along Lower Castle Street and turn left into QUAKERS' FRIARS(T).

A Dominican Friary was founded here by Maurice of Gaunt in 1227. After the dissolution of the monasteries by Henry VIII, it was used by the Guilds of Bakers and Cutlers, two of the medieval craft guilds which regulated trade in Bristol. The friary was later bought by the Society of Friends — the Quakers — and was their home from 1670 to 1956. William Penn, a Quaker and founder of Pennsylvania, was married here to Susan Callowhill.

Part of the present building was built by George Tully in 1747. It now houses the Registrar for Births, Marriages and Deaths.

Leave Quakers' Friars on the northern side and enter the Broadmead Shopping Precinct. Near the entrance to the Lower Arcade is the NEW ROOM(U), also known as John Wesley's Chapel, the oldest Methodist building in the world.

After a period as missionaries in Georgia, John and Charles Wesley returned to Britain and John reluctantly accepted an invitation from George Whitefield to visit Bristol and to continue his ministry in the city and to the colliers of Kingswood. A plaque in Old Bread Street marks the site where, for the first time in this country, John Wesley preached in the open air.

His success led to the building in 1739 of 'our New Room in the Horsefair'. It became a centre for Bible exposition and preaching, the teaching of children and the giving of medical help to the sick. It was enlarged in 1748. After the death of John Wesley, the building was owned for over 100 years by Welsh Calvinistic Methodists, before being restored to Wesleyan Methodists, now the Methodist Church.

The Presbyterian Church of Wales still holds regular Welsh services. There is no regular English congregation, but special services are held from time to time.

An equestrian statue of John Wesley in the forecourt faces Broadmead and nearby is a stable for the preacher's horse. Wesley travelled over 250,000 miles during 50 years of preaching in the open air. From this chapel in 1771 he sent Francis Astbury, one of his preachers, to America. There are

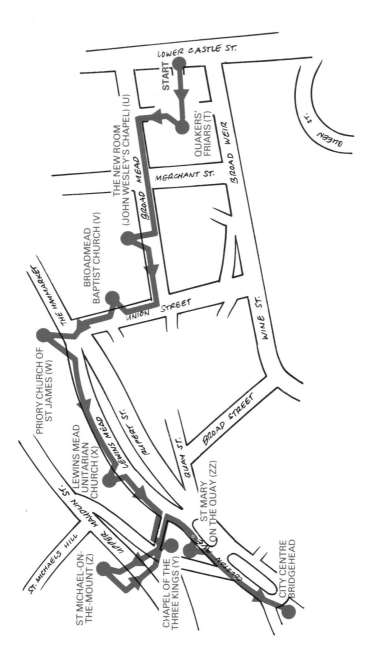

LOWER CASTLE ST.

START

QUAKERS' FRIARS (T)

BROAD WEIR

QUEEN ST.

THE NEW ROOM (JOHN WESLEY'S CHAPEL) (U)

BROAD MEAD

MERCHANT ST.

BROADMEAD BAPTIST CHURCH (V)

THE HAYMARKET

UNION STREET

WINE ST.

PRIORY CHURCH OF ST JAMES (W)

LEWINS MEAD UNITARIAN CHURCH (X)

LEWINS MEAD

RUPERT ST.

QUAY ST.

BROAD STREET

ST. MICHAELS HILL ST.

MAUDLIN ST.

UPPER

ST MARY ON THE QUAY (ZZ)

ST MICHAEL-ON-THE-MOUNT (Z)

CHAPEL OF THE THREE KINGS (Y)

COLSTON AVE.

CITY CENTRE BRIDGEHEAD

The New Room *The equestrian statue of John Wesley, erected to mark his years of itinerant preaching.*

now over 26 million Methodists there and 55 million worldwide and it all began in the New Room, Bristol.

The Room contains a fine two–decker **Pulpit** and a **Communion Table** which was made in about 1760.

The **Organ** is the work of a noted builder named Johann Snetzler. It was originally erected in a Norfolk church in 1760 and moved to its present position in 1930. Above the

The New Room *The interior, with the two-decker pulpit.*

chapel are the domestic rooms of John Wesley and his preachers with many exhibits associated with their life and ministry.

On the other side of the building is a statue of John's brother, Charles, who ministered in the New Room and lived in nearby Charles Street. He wrote over 6,000 hymns, some of which are still popular today.

Both brothers always maintained loyalty to the Church of England and, with the New Room congregation, worshipped regularly at St James' (a later stop on our tour). *Open: Monday–Saturday, 10am–4pm, except Bank Holidays and winter Wednesdays.*

Returning to Broadmead, turn right and right again at the next corner, to arrive at BROADMEAD BAPTIST CHURCH(V) which is above a row of shops, as were former churches.

The congregation first occupied this site in 1672 when they took possession of upper rooms previously occupied by the Quakers. The early days of the congregation were carefully recorded by one of the founding elders, Edward Terrill, in what has become known as the 'Broadmead Records'.

The original church was built in 1693 and enlarged and rebuilt several times up to 1877. This was replaced in 1967—69 by a modern suite of buildings with shops at ground level and the church and ancillary accommodation at 1st and 2nd floor levels.

One feature of the church is the **Rope Handrail** attached to the wall of the stairs leading to the 1st floor concourse. This is a reminder of the days when Baptists were persecuted. Look-outs at the door pulled on the rope as a warning that bailiffs were approaching, whereupon the preacher would escape, either disguised as a member of the congregation or, as legend has it, through a secret door in the pulpit. The ladies of the congregation held on to the rope as they stood on the stairs to impede the access of the bailiffs.

On the first floor are memorials which tell stories of the difficulties faced by early Baptists. Many preachers spent long periods in jail. Whilst there, one of them contrived to preach through the bars of his cell to his congregation. *Open: daily, 9.30am—4.30pm.*

Turn right and cross the roundabout to the churchyard of the PRIORY CHURCH OF ST JAMES(W), founded in 1129 as a cell of the Benedictine Abbey of Tewkesbury by Robert, Earl of Gloucester. He was buried in the east end of the church, which was destroyed at the dissolution of the monasteries. The church is now closed to visitors.

Originally there were cloisters, refectory, dormitory and chapter house, but only the chapel remains. The west end of the church is notable for the **Wheel Window**, though it has suffered much wear through the ages, and for the row of intersecting arches.

St James' became a parish church in 1374. The south aisle was made wider in the late 17th century, but the inner north aisle is still as it was in Norman times, when it adjoined the monks' cloister. The Perpendicular tower was built at the end of the 14th century and contains the original peal of bells. The timber roof with stone corbels was installed at the same time.

Eleanor of Brittany was buried in the priory in 1241. She had been imprisoned in Bristol Castle by her brother King John (1199—1216) so that she could not produce an heir to the English throne and threaten his dynasty. She died childless and was later re-buried in a nunnery at Amesbury.

St. James' *The east end (J. Trelawny-Ross).*

St James' was the parish church of the Wesleys, and the only remaining gravestone in the churchyard is that of five infant children and an adult daughter of Charles Wesley.

Around the corner, on Lower Maudlin Street, is the White Hart Hotel which, from 1480, was the guest house of the Priory. The cellars date to the foundation of the Priory in the 12th century. They are said to be haunted by a ghost 'kept sweet as long as there are flowers in the house'.

From St James', Lewin's Mead leads back towards the Centre. On it are two modern office blocks named Grey Friars and White Friars in memory of members of the Franciscan and Carmelite communities who lived close by.

On the right, is the former LEWINS MEAD UNITARIAN CHURCH(X) which is conspicuous for its fine semi-circular porch and Ionic columns. Though now used for business purposes, it is well preserved. It was originally built in 1694 as an Independent Meeting House, and was rebuilt in 1791 by the Unitarians.

Further along, there is an impressive ancient gateway which once led to the Hospital of St Bartholomew, founded in the early 13th century for the care of the poor. Just inside is a statue of the 'Mother and Child', probably from the Carmelite Friary. In 1352, the Hospital became the first home of the Bristol Grammar School and later, it housed Queen Elizabeth's Hospital.

If you have the time and energy for a diversion, take a narrow alley on the right and climb Christmas Steps, formerly called Knifesmith's Street and the start of the road to Wales. It was 'steppered down and finished in 1669' and is now lined with fascinating shops.

At the top stands the CHAPEL OF THE THREE KINGS(Y) (1504), serving Foster's Almshouses. The inspiration for the dedication came to John Foster, its founder, when he was trading up the river Rhine and visited Cologne Cathedral. The statues of Caspar, Melchior and Balthazar are by the modern Bristol artist, Ernest Pascoe. (The key to the chapel can be obtained from the warden of the almshouses).

Further up the hill is the CHURCH OF ST MICHAEL-ON-THE-MOUNT-WITHOUT(Z). The original church was built in 1147 by Robert Fitzhamon, founder of Tewkesbury Abbey, of which it was a tributary. As the name implies, the church stood outside the city walls. The original church was rebuilt in the 15th century and, once again, in 1775 (although the 15th century tower was retained). It stands on the hill which the Protestant Marian martyrs climbed on their way to execution. Sir Michael Redgrave, the actor, was born in theatrical digs overlooking the Church.
Open: Tuesday and Thursday, 11am–3pm, Saturday, 9am–noon.

Close by is Tankards Close. Originally it was called Stinkards Close, appropriately enough, since it was built on the site of a plague pit.

Near the foot of the hill is the King David's Hotel, which stands on the site of the Nunnery of St Mary Magdalene. Sponsored by the wife of the founder of the Cathedral, they

Chapel of the Three Kings (*J. Trelawny-Ross*).

were known as the White Ladies, which may be the origin of the name of Whiteladies Road, a main road bordering Clifton. During the Black Death (1348), when hundreds of people were dying in Bedminster and boatmen refused to cross the river, the nuns rowed themselves over, and died while trying to help the victims.

Return down Christmas Steps, turn right, and you come to ST MARY ON THE QUAY(ZZ), built in 1840 by the Irvingites in neo-classical style with a six-columned Corinthian portico. Originally it stood on the waterfront where

St. Mary on the Quay (*J. Trelawny-Ross*).

ships were constantly moored. Now the river runs in a culvert under the Centre.

The church was later taken over in 1843 by the Roman Catholic Church and is served by priests of the Society of Jesus. The interior boasts a gallery at the west end and a very serene treatment of the east end. The entrance to the sanctuary is flanked by a pair of superb Corinthian columns. *Open: Monday–Saturday, c.8.30am–6pm, Sunday, 7.30am–noon, 2.30pm–6pm.*

Continue towards the Bridgehead. On the right is the Colston Hall, Bristol's premier concert venue. It is built on the site of a Carmelite Friary which had the largest Friary church in Bristol. It had a tall, slender steeple, 200ft high, and a nave 90ft long.

Further on is the Bridgehead, from where we started this tour.

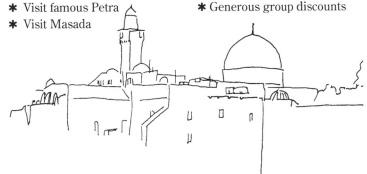

CLIFTON AND WESTBURY

Best taken by car, although the Clifton section makes a pleasant walk. The No 8 bus takes a circular route from College Green to Clifton Cathedral and Christ Church.

Starting from College Green, proceed up Park Street. Take the second turning on the left into Great George Street, which leads up Brandon Hill. ST GEORGE'S CHURCH(AA), on the right, was built to commemorate the Battle of Waterloo. Because of its excellent acoustics, it is now used for musical concerts and music recording sessions by the BBC. Opposite is the Georgian House Museum, a typical merchant's house, built in 1789. It was here that the poets Wordsworth and Coleridge met for the first time.

At the top of Park Street stands the University Tower, a neo-Gothic building presented to the University by Sir George Wills, a member of the tobacco family. It was designed by Sir George Oatley and opened in 1925. Next to it is the City Museum and Art Gallery.

Following the traffic around the Triangle, you come to the Victoria Rooms, an impressive colonnaded building that belongs to the University and is a conference centre. Pass to the left of the Victoria Rooms and take the third turning on the right into Pembroke Road.

On the left, within a short distance, stands the modern CATHEDRAL OF ST PETER AND ST PAUL(AB), consecrated in 1973. It is the home of the Roman Catholic Diocese of Clifton and is an outstanding example of modernist church architecture. Special care was taken to serve the requirements of the newest forms of liturgical worship. As a result, the architects were awarded the Bronze Medal of the Royal Institution of British Architects when it was completed.

The three impressive glass doors incorporate the Coat of Arms of the City of Bristol and the Diocese of Clifton. Both Coats of Arms were presented by the City of Bristol.

The **Narthex** (entrance hall) contains two stained glass windows by Henry Haig called 'Pentecost' and 'Jubilation'. Over 8000 pieces of glass were used in their construction. In the **Baptistery**, the font is the work of Simon Verity of Malmesbury and is carved from Portland Stone (the base) and Spangled Purbeck (the bowl). The fish, carved inside

St. George's *Southern approach steps: the Samuel Jackson drawing, 1825 (City Art Gallery).*

the bowl, is the ancient symbol of Christ, and the doves on the base represent the Holy Spirit. The words inscribed around the rim are taken from Peter 2:10. Set into the wall near the font are the Holy Oils used in the Sacraments of Baptism, Confirmation, Ordination, and the Anointing of the Sick.

The seating in the **Nave** is arranged so that no person is more than 50ft from the **Altar**, which is placed in front of the Sanctuary so as to appear in the midst of the worshippers. It is hewn from Portland Stone. The candlesticks, designed by the architects (the Percy Thomas Partnership)

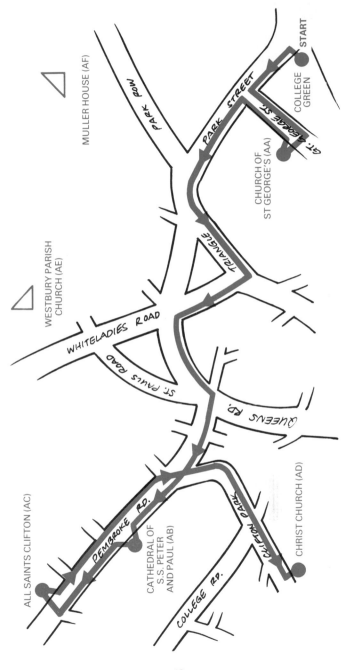

MULLER HOUSE (AF)

PARK ROW

PARK STREET

GT. GEORGE ST.

START

COLLEGE GREEN

CHURCH OF ST GEORGE'S (AA)

TRIANGLE

WESTBURY PARISH CHURCH (AE)

WHITELADIES ROAD

ST. PAULS ROAD

QUEENS RD.

ALL SAINTS CLIFTON (AC)

PEMBROKE RD.

CATHEDRAL OF S.S. PETER AND PAUL (AB)

COLLEGE RD.

CLIFTON PARK

CHRIST CHURCH (AD)

Clifton Cathedral (*J. Trelawny-Ross*).

Simon Verity's font, with Henry Haig windows behind.

69

are simple so as not to detract from the silver candlesticks designed by Stephanie Gilbert. The lectern was made by William Mitchell to the architects' design.

Around the nave are the **Stations of the Cross**. Designed by William Mitchell, they depict various events in the passion of Our Lord.

1. The Last Supper.
2. Jesus prays in the garden.
3. Jesus is betrayed and arrested.
4. Jesus is disowned by Peter.
5. Jesus is scourged and mocked.
6. Jesus is condemned to death.
7. Jesus falls under his Cross.
8. Jesus is helped by Simon of Cyrene.
9. Jesus meets the women of Jersualem.
10. Jesus is nailed to the Cross.
11. Jesus speaks to his mother.
12. Jesus forgives the repentant thief.
13. Jesus dies on the cross.
14. Jesus is Risen.

The Organ, built by Rieger Orgelbau of Austria, has tracker section and is of fine workmanship. The casework is ash and the pipes are made chiefly of tin.

The **Blessed Sacrament Chapel** serves as a place of

One of William Mitchell's Stations of the Cross.

The Lady Statue, in bronze, by Terry Jones.

private prayer and the celebration of weekday Masses. The Tabernacle is made of stainless steel, the work of John Alder, and is used for the reservation of the Eucharist for the sick. Its form is repeated in the red lamp. The ambulatory screen was made at Prinknash Abbey and is a gift from the monks there. On the rear wall is a painting of the Crucifixion, in the Spanish tradition, by the local artist James Scrase. It was presented by the La Retraite School Old Girls' Society.

The Lady Chapel contains a bronze statue of Mary, Mother of the Lord, by Terry Jones.

Two of the bells and some important brass tablets outlin-

All Saints', Clifton *Rebuilt after war damage, a striking combination of the old and the new (J. Trelawny-Ross).*

ing the history of the Bishops of Clifton come from the former pro-cathedral.
Open: daily, 9am–7pm.

A little further up Pembroke Road is the church of ALL SAINTS', CLIFTON(AC). The original church was the work of the noted Victorian architect G E Street, who also designed the nave of Bristol Cathedral. It was rebuilt after being mostly destroyed by incendiary bombs on the night of December 2nd, 1940. The new church was consecrated on July 1st, 1967. It is a striking combination of old and new, the work of architect Robert Potter. The war memorial outside and some notable furnishings are by F.C. Eden, and the modern stained glass windows are by John Piper. The tower of the old church serves as a porch and houses one bell, which came from St Augustine's on College Green. It is inscribed 'Cast by Wm Evans of Chepstow, 1739. Success to the Trade of Bristol'.

Open: daily, 7am–6pm.

Christ Church, Clifton *(J. Trelawny-Ross)*.

Go back along Pembroke Road past Clifton Cathedral, then turn right into Clifton Park. A short distance along, where the Downs meet the houses of Clifton, stands CHRIST CHURCH(AD), built on a grassy platform which enhances its beauty. It was consecrated in 1844. The tower and spire were built by John Norton in 1859 and the aisles were added in the 1880s. The church is noted for its fine musical tradition.

Open: Sunday services. The church interior can be viewed during daylight hours from the vestibule.

Brunel's Clifton Suspension Bridge is a very short distance from the Church and should not be missed.

On the north east side of the Downs is the village of Westbury-on-Trym. During the 10th and 11th centuries it was within the Diocese of Worcester, where St Wulfstan was bishop. He visited Bristol and strongly denounced the people for selling English children into slavery in Ireland. He was so greatly respected for his humility and asceticism that he was one of the very few bishops allowed to retain his see when the Normans arrived.

In 720, the Abbess Ciolburga, Mother Superior of a convent at Berkeley, was given a nunnery by her son. It must have existed for some time previously. On her death, the convent passed into the control of the Bishop of Worcester, an inheritance which was confirmed by a convocation of clergy in 824. The convent was destroyed by Danish invaders.

The origins of the PARISH CHURCH(AE) go back further than any church in the city except Pip 'n Jay. From 962 it was, for a time, a Benedictine community until the monks moved to Ramsey. Some of the church dates from soon after 1200. Mostly, however, it is Perpendicular, some of it added by Bishop Carpenter of Worcester, who hoped that it would become a second cathedral in his diocese. His tomb is in the choir.

An unusual feature is the 15th century **Apse**. The peal of bells is claimed to be amongst the best in the country.

In the **Lady Chapel** is a modern figure of the Blessed Virgin carved in the Walsingham style.

Open: daily, 9am–6pm.

74

The college, home of the clergy and centre of studies, was some way from the church beside the River Trym. Only the gate tower and two corner turrets remain.

Those interested in the work of George Müller might like to return to the Centre by way of Cotham Park to visit MÜLLER HOUSE(AF) the centre of activities by the George Müller Foundation.

Müller House is open from 9 am to 5 pm from Monday to Friday when the staff will be pleased to welcome Old Boys and Girls as well as other visitors. There is a small museum of memorabilia and, of course, full information about the current work. If possible, please advise them of your visit in advance.

Formerly housed in three large homes at Ashley Down the Foundation has considerably de-centralised its work into smaller communities for children and the elderly in need, and in supporting the work of the Scriptural Knowledge Institutions abroad. The Foundation also operates E C L Bookshops at Park Street, Bristol and in Bath and Weston-super-Mare.

One aspect remains unchanged from the days of George Müller. The Homes make no appeals for funds; yet, through unswerving faith in God, money is received almost daily to continue the work started by George Müller in Bristol in 1836.

Open: Monday–Friday, 9am–5pm.

ARCHITECTURAL NOTES

NORMAN (Romanesque)
c 1066—1200

Characterised by massive walls and columns which are needed to support round arches.

Vaulted stone roofs were normally barrel shaped. Exceptionally, as in the Bristol Cathedral chapter house, diagonally intersecting ribs vaults were used.

Door arches were made up of overlapping rings, each supported by a vertical shaft. Important arches were ornately carved. Because the carving was normally done with an axe, it featured geometrical patterns such as zig-zag.

Windows were very thin, deep set, and rounded.

Examples

Bristol Cathedral:	Gatehouse Arch, Lower Gateway to school, Chapter House vestibule
St Mary Redcliffe:	Inner north porch
St James' Priory:	Five western bays in nave
All Saints':	West nave

GOTHIC

EARLY ENGLISH c 1200—1275

Typified by narrow pointed arches and windows (lancets). Pointed arches meant that greater heights could be achieved. Weight was carried to the ground through external buttresses which were normally placed two to a corner at right angles.

Lancet windows were placed singly or in twos or threes (as Bristol Cathedral).

Examples

Bristol Cathedral:	Elder Lady Chapel
St Philip & St Jacob:	South transept tower
St Mark's (Lord Mayor's Chapel):	Main aisle

The arch became wider and less pointed. Two or three lancet windows were combined under one frame and separated by ribs called mullions. These mullions increasingly formed patterned networks called *tracery*. Exterior arches of windows and doors were protected by an upper arch called a *dripstone*. The ballflower (a kind of circular opening bud) ornament was often used.

Roofs were mainly of timber. Stone vaults were used in more important buildings (such as the Cathedral). Normally, there would be a long *ridge rib* running from east to west at the highest point intersected by diagonal ribs. More decorative *lierne ribs* were, however, pioneered in Bristol Cathedral. Carved bosses were placed at the intersection of the ribs.

Examples

Bristol Cathedral:	Choir
	Eastern Lady Chapel
St Stephen's:	Base of north aisle
St Mark's (Lord Mayor's Chapel):	Main aisle
St Nicholas:	Crypt
St Mary Redcliffe:	The Outer North Porch
St Philip & St Jacob:	Aisles and main church
St James' Priory:	Pillars and west window
	North aisle

PERPENDICULAR c 1375—1510

Windows and arches became wider and flatter. Windows become 'walls of glass' and are most recognisable for straight mullions which go vertically from top to bottom of the window. Most major churches had a *clerestory*: a row of windows at second floor level around the nave and chancel. Roof vaults were called *fan vaults* and were delicate, intricate and complex.

Examples

St Mark's (Lord Mayor's Chapel):	Pointz Chapel and East End
All Saints:	East nave
Temple:	Tower
St James':	Tower
St Stephen's:	Main roof
St Mary Redcliffe	Eastern Lady Chapel, clerestory, chancel and transepts
St Thomas the Martyr:	Tower & timber roof
Westbury-on-Trym Parish Church:	Main part of church

OPENING HOURS

All Saints'	Monday—Friday (School term time only), 11am—3pm.
All Saints', Clifton	Daily, 7am—6pm.
Bristol Cathedral	Daily, 8am—6pm. Lunches and snacks served in the Buttery from 10am to 4pm Monday to Saturday. Traditional carvery lunch from noon to 2pm on Sunday.
Broadmead Baptist	Daily, 9.30am—4.30pm.
Cathedral of SS Peter and Paul	Daily, 9am—7pm.
Chapel of the Three Kings	The key can be obtained from the warden of the almshouses.
Christ Church	Monday—Friday, 7.30am—5pm, and Sunday services.
Christ Church, Clifton	Sunday services. The church interior can be viewed during daylight hours from the vestibule.
Muller House	Monday—Friday, 9am—5pm.
Lewin's Mead Unitarian	Used for business purposes.
The New Room	Monday—Saturday 10am—4pm, except Bank Holidays and winter Wednesdays.
St George's	Open only during concerts.
St James' Priory	Not open to the public.
St John's	Tuesday & Thursday, noon—3pm.
St Mark's (Lord Mayor's Chapel)	Daily (except Monday) 10am—noon, 1pm—4pm, and Sunday services.
St Mary on the Quay	Monday—Saturday c.8.30am—6pm, Sunday 7.30am—noon, 2.30pm—6pm.
St Mary Redcliffe	Daily, 8am—5pm.
St Michael-on-the-Mount-Without	Tuesday & Thursday, 11am—3pm, Saturday 9am—noon.
St Nicholas Church Museum	Telephone City Museum (223571) for current opening times.
St Philip's and St Jacob's	Tuesday & Thursday, 12noon—2pm (lunches are served). Sunday, 10am—6.30pm. Also open by appointment — tel 243169 in advance.
St Stephen's	Monday—Friday, 7.30am—5pm, and Sunday services.
St Thomas the Martyr	Closed.
Westbury Parish Church	Daily 9am—6pm.

Bristol City Docks
A Guide to the
Historic Harbour

Walks around the waterfront. Maps, photographs and listings make this the essential reference to what to see and do in the area.

£2.95